DEAR *you*

tHANK YOU

BY
Robie Rogge

UNION
SQUARE
& CO.

NEW YORK

A simple "THANK YOU" is not enough
to express my gratitude to you for:

_____

With an abundance of appreciation,

TO: _____

FROM: _____

DATE: _____

I can no
other answer
make but
THANKS,
and
THANKS;
and ever
THANKS.

———

William Shakespeare

tHaNK YOu!

I hope this book, with over 100 expressions of gratitude, will top even William Shakespeare in conveying to you my own thanks.

Collected here are expressions of gratitude from presidents, writers, scientists, philosophers, artists, and statesmen. Some of the contributors are thankful for the simple pleasures of friendship—sharing a glass of water or being able to call someone at 4 a.m. On a grander scale, others express an appreciation of art, which expands our vision of the universe, or give thanks to heroes and "she-roes," or pay tribute to a great teacher.

The quotations are curated and paired to provide sources of wisdom, reflection, and entertainment: Anita Loos extols the euphoria produced by a cup of coffee, while Sydney Smith, on the facing page, is glad he was not born before tea. Kathleen Norris describes a perfect feast; Benjamin Disraeli, meanwhile, puzzles over an unusual sensation, which if not indigestion "must be gratitude." Several pairs praise the talent of gift-giving (Ovid even claims that giving calls for genius!).

Interspersed among these pairs of quotes are some longer letters of thanks: Barack Obama's letter to a constituent thanking him for the privilege of serving as his president; Jane Austen's gratitude to an early reader of *Emma*, whose praise assured Austen that she hadn't "overwritten myself"; and a letter from the young Frédéric Chopin to his papa, expressing his utmost gratitude and filial affection in words, because notes of music were not adequate.

There should be enough versions of "thank you" in this book to match my own. But I hope you will not be tempted to follow Evelyn Waugh's father, who in the last 20 years of his life wrote thank-you notes for thank-you notes, and the chain was not broken until his death.

NO BETTER WORDS THAN "THANK YOU" HAVE YET BEEN DISCOVERED to express the sincere gratitude of one's heart, when the two words are sincerely spoken.

—

Alfred Armand Montapert

" *Thank you.* "

I've said thank you thousands of times in my life. Most of the time I mean it to some degree. **There are times when I've said it and felt the gratitude behind the words wholeheartedly,** but I don't think I ever understood what those two words truly meant until this very moment. **Now I think I need a new phrase because thank you is insufficient in this situation.**

* * * * * *

KIM HOLDEN

Let us be grateful to the people who make us happy; they are the charming gardeners who make our souls blossom.

Marcel Proust

Friendships
MULTIPLY JOYS
✖ *and* ÷
DIVIDE GRIEFS.

—

Thomas Fuller

*Give thanks
for a little,
and you will
find a lot.*

—

HAUSA PROVERB

No act of kindness, no matter how small, is ever wasted.

———

Aesop

Giving presents is a talent; to know what a person wants, to know when and how to get it, to give it lovingly and well.

—

Pamela Glenconner

Giving
calls for
genius.

OVID

Of all things
which **wisdom**
provides to
make us
entirely happy,
much the
greatest is
the possession of
friendship.

—

EPICURUS

With true friends . . . even water drunk
together is sweet enough.

—

CHINESE PROVERB

Accept my thanks for... your kind deposition in favour of Emma. In my present state of doubt as to her reception in the world, it is particularly gratifying to me to receive so early an assurance of your Ladyship's approbation. It encourages me to *depend on the same share of general good opinion which Emma's predecessors have experienced, and to believe that I have not yet, as almost every writer of fancy does sooner or later, overwritten myself.*

Letter from novelist **JANE AUSTEN** to the Countess of Morley, author and illustrator, December 31, 1851

When I wake up
every morning,
I smile and say,
"Thank you."
Because out of my
window I can see
the mountains,
then go hiking
with my dog
and share her
bounding joy in
the world.

—

CAROLE KING

Animals are such agreeable friends—they ask no questions, they pass no criticisms.

—

George Eliot

Only through art
can we get outside of
ourselves and know
another's view
of the universe which is
not the same as ours and
see landscapes which
would otherwise have
remained unknown
to us like
the landscapes of the
moon. Thanks to art,
instead of seeing a single
world, our own, we see
it multiply until we have
before us as many worlds
as there are
original artists.

—

Marcel Proust

MUSIC, because of its specific and far-reaching metaphorical powers— can name the unnamable and communicate the unknowable.

———

Leonard Bernstein

The feast had
all the elements of
perfection: good
company, firelight,
and appetite.

—

KATHLEEN NORRIS

I feel a very
unusual
SENSATION—
if it is not
indigestion,
I think it must
be **GRATITUDE**.

—

BENJAMIN DISRAELI

**We make a living
by what we get;**
we make a life by
what we give.

ANONYMOUS

No person was ever honored for what he **RECEIVED**. **HONOR** has been the reward for what he **GAVE**.

—

CALVIN COOLIDGE

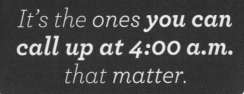

It's the ones **you can call up at 4:00 a.m.** that matter.

—

MARLENE DIETRICH

A real friend is one who walks **IN** when the rest of the world walks **OUT**.

—

Walter Winchell

DEAR PAPA!

I could express my feelings more easily if they could be put into notes of music, but as the very best concert would not cover my affection for you, dear Daddy,

I must use the simple words from my heart, to lay before you my utmost gratitude and filial affection.

Letter from the composer **FRÉDÉRIC CHOPIN** to his father on his name-day, December 6, 1818

MY MISERY LOVED YOUR COMPANY.

Thanks for being there.

ANONYMOUS

Some people
go to **priests**;
others to **poetry**;
I to **my friends.**

VIRGINIA WOOLF

The best things in life are not things.

———

GINNY MOORE

A **SINGLE** conversation across the table with a wise man **IS WORTH A MONTH'S STUDY OF BOOKS.**

CHINESE PROVERB

I SUPPOSE *there is one friend in the life of each of us who seems not a separate person, however dear and beloved, but an expansion, an interpretation, of one's self, the very meaning of one's soul.*

—

EDITH WHARTON

*She is a friend
of my mind.*

SHE GATHER ME, MAN.

The pieces **I AM,**
*she gather them
and give them back
to me in all*
THE RIGHT ORDER.

—

Toni Morrison

'Tis not the **FOOD,**
but the **CONTENT,**
That makes the table's
MERRIMENT.

* * * * * * * * * * * *

Robert Herrick

It isn't so much
what's on
the table that
matters, as
what's on the
chairs.

W. S. GILBERT

At times, our own
light goes out and is
rekindled by a spark from
another person. Each of
us has cause to think with
deep gratitude of those
who have lighted the
flame within us.

———

ALBERT SCHWEITZER

NO ONE WHO **ACHIEVES SUCCESS** DOES SO WITHOUT THE HELP OF **OTHERS.**

THE WISE AND CONFIDENT ACKNOWLEDGE THIS HELP **WITH GRATITUDE.**

—

Alfred North Whitehead

YOUR CHARMING

remembrance of me on my birthday—the jolly, round, and happy little monk bedded in flowers, came safely in the wooden cradle.... I am ashamed to send back the basket, or bucket empty; but I look round in vain for something to fill it.

What shall I do?
After all, the greatest grace of a gift, perhaps, is that it anticipates and admits of no return. I therefore accept yours, pure and simple; and on the whole am glad that I have nothing to send back in the basket.

Letter from poet **HENRY WADSWORTH LONGFELLOW** to Mrs. J. T. Fields, author and Boston literary hostess, February 28, 1871

Thank you for helping me **understand** that there's nothing wrong in loving **darkness**, in being quiet. Nothing to lose by being an introvert.

—

NITYA PRAKASH

Oh, the comfort—
the inexpressible comfort
of feeling safe with a person,
having neither to weigh
thoughts, nor measure words,
but pouring them all out, just as
they are, *chaff and grain together;*
knowing that a faithful hand
will take and sift them—keep what
is worth keeping—and with
the breath of kindness
blow the rest away.

—

Dinah Mulock Craik

THE BEST
way to pay
for a lovely
moment is to
ENJOY IT.

—

RICHARD BACH

We can only
be said to be alive in
those moments when
*our hearts are conscious
of our treasures.*

—

THORNTON WILDER

"Someday you'll remember what I said and you will thank me for it. Francie wished adults would stop telling her that. Already the load of thanks in the future was weighing her down.

—

BETTY SMITH

**The one prediction
that never comes true is,**

"You'll thank
me for telling
you this."

JUDITH MARTIN

HOW **IMPORTANT** IT IS FOR US TO RECOGNIZE AND CELEBRATE OUR **HEROES** AND **SHE-ROES.**

—

Maya Angelou

None of us got where we are solely by pulling ourselves up by our bootstraps. We got there because somebody—a parent, a teacher, an Ivy League crony or a few nuns— bent down and helped us pick up our boots.

——

Thurgood Marshall

A trusty companion
HALVES
the journey and
DOUBLES
the courage.

—

EDWARD BULWER-LYTTON

There is no *satisfaction* in any good without a *companion.*

SENECA THE YOUNGER

I *want to thank you* for the dresses. They are first very pretty, and second a good fit and third something that I could not have bought for myself. But greatest of all I am joyful because your generosity has made me bloom like the desert after a rain. I am not forgetting for a single second the part my Godmother played in my good fortune, but I do not wish to fall short in my appreciation of your kindness either. I look very beautiful in the dresses and you will perhaps feel a tiny twinge of jealousy when you gaze upon me, but the artist in you will be so delighted at the sight of such a perfect union of clothes and woman that you will stifle your jealousy at once and rejoice with me. *Thanks and thanks and thanks.*

Letter from author **ZORA NEALE HURSTON** to Cornelia Chapin, sculptor, February 29, 1932

I would
maintain that
thanks are the
highest form
of thought; and
that **GRATITUDE
IS HAPPINESS**
doubled by
wonder.

* * * * * * * * *

G. K. CHESTERTON

IT IS NOT JOY
THAT MAKES US
GRATEFUL; IT
IS GRATITUDE
THAT MAKES US
JOYFUL. ♥

****

DAVID STEINDL-RAST

*There are people whom **one loves** immediately and **forever.** Even to know they are alive in the world with one is **quite enough.***

———

NANCY SPAIN

BEAUTIFUL AND RICH
is an old friendship, / Grateful
to the touch as ancient ivory, /
Smooth as aged wine, or sheen
of tapestry / Where light has
lingered, intimate and long. /
Full of tears and warm is an old
friendship. / That asks no longer
deeds of gallantry, / Or any deed
at all—save that the friend
shall be / Alive and
breathing somewhere,
LIKE A SONG.

—

EUNICE TIETJENS

We pray for the **BIG THINGS** and forget to give thanks for **the ordinary,** small (and yet really not small) gifts.

—

Dietrich Bonhoeffer

To do something however **small,** to make others

HAPPIER

and better, is the **highest**

AMBITION,

the most **elevating** hope,
which can inspire a

HUMAN BEING.

———

John Lubbock

Better than a **THOUSAND DAYS** of diligent study is one day with a **GREAT TEACHER.**

—

JAPANESE PROVERB

A teacher affects eternity; *he can never tell where his influence stops.*

HENRY ADAMS

Wherever
you are it is your
own friends who
make your world.

—

WILLIAM JAMES

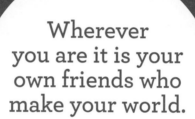

➤➤ **The only** ←←
people with whom
you should try to get
even are those who
have helped you.

———

JOHN E. SOUTHARD

Allow me to thank you, as I certainly do thank you most sincerely for your thoughtful kindness in making me the owner of a cane which was formerly the property and the favorite walking staff of your late lamented husband the honored and venerated President of the United States. I assure you, that this inestimable memento of his Excellency will be retained in my possession while I live—an object of sacred interest—a token not merely of the kind consideration in which I have reason to know that the President was pleased to hold me personally, but as an indication of his humane interest in the welfare of my whole race.

Letter from abolitionist FREDERICK DOUGLASS to Mary Todd Lincoln, the widow of President Abraham Lincoln, August 17, 1865

WE MUST FIND TIME TO STOP AND THANK **THE PEOPLE** WHO MAKE A DIFFERENCE **IN OUR LIVES.**

—

JOHN F. KENNEDY

You are part
of my **STORY,**
MEMORY and
SCENERY,
thank you.

—

KIM TAEHYUNG

I ALWAYS FELT ↑ that the great high privilege, relief and comfort of friendship was that one had to explain nothing.

—

Katherine Mansfield

Flowers are lovely;
Love is flower-like;
Friendship is
a sheltering tree.

—

SAMUEL TAYLOR COLERIDGE

Some find their
heroes 'mid the
battle's strife;
*The greatest heroes
are in private life.*

———

SIMEON CARTER

THE WORK AN
UNKNOWN GOOD
MAN HAS DONE IS
LIKE A VEIN OF
WATER FLOWING
HIDDEN UNDERGROUND,
SECRETLY MAKING
THE GROUND GREEN.

Thomas Carlyle

How far that little candle throws his beams! **SO SHINES A GOOD DEED** *in a naughty world.*

———

WILLIAM
SHAKESPEARE

Gratitude
can transform
common days into
thanksgivings,
turn routine jobs
into joy, and
change ordinary
opportunities into
blessings.

———

William Arthur Ward

Life is to be fortified by many friendships.

To love, and to be loved, is the greatest happiness of existence.

Sidney Smith

Pleasure is necessarily **RECIPROCAL**; no one feels [it], who does not at the same time give it. To be pleased, **ONE MUST PLEASE.**

—

Lord Chesterfield

THANK YOU
- - - - - - - - - - - - - -
*for your letter; it
was as pleasant
as a quiet chat,
as welcome as
spring showers,*

as reviving as a friend's visit; in short, it was very like a page of Cranford....

Letter from novelist and poet **Charlotte Brontë** to Mrs. Elizabeth Gaskell, author of *Cranford*, and Brontë's biographer, July 9, 1853

One can never thank people, *I thought regretfully, at least not by piling gratitude on top of them like heavy American Beauty roses. One can never pay in gratitude;* one can only pay "in kind" *somewhere else in life.*

—

ANNE MORROW LINDBERGH

Every action of your life touches on some chord that will vibrate in eternity.

EDWIN HUBBELL CHAPIN

GOOD COMPANY, *lively conversation, and the endearments of friendship fill the mind with great pleasure.*

EDMUND BURKE

THE KEY IS TO KEEP COMPANY ONLY WITH PEOPLE WHO UPLIFT YOU, WHOSE PRESENCE CALLS FORTH YOUR BEST.

EPICTETUS

"Thank YOU,"

is the best prayer that anyone could say. I say that one a lot. Thank you expresses extreme gratitude, humility, understanding.

—

ALICE WALKER

A
JOYFUL
≫≫→ and ←≪≪
PLEASANT
thing it is to be
THANKFUL.

—

PSALM 147

Not what we give, but what we share—for the gift without the giver is bare.

—

JAMES RUSSELL LOWELL

The manner of
GIVING
is worth

more than the
GIFT.

—

PIERRE CORNEILLE

"THANKS FOR THE MEMORY"

—

Song title,
lyrics by LEO ROBIN

God gave us **memories** that we might have roses in December.

J. M. Barrie

On the final night of my Presidency, I read the handwritten card you sent me, and I wanted to reach out to thank you. Your kind words were deeply moving, and while I appreciate your thinking of me, please know the honor was all mine—it was the privilege of my life to serve as your President. There are certainly milestone moments we will always

remember from the past
eight years, but for me, it
was hearing from people
like you that kept me
going every single day.
My heart has been touched
time and again by the
daily acts of kindness that
embody the American
people at their core, and
as I take some time now to
rest and reflect on all we
have achieved together,
know that your thoughtful
gesture will stay with me.

Letter from PRESIDENT BARACK OBAMA
to a well-wisher, June 19, 2017

To send a letter is
a good way to go
somewhere *without
moving anything but
your heart.*

PHYLLIS THEROUX

Messenger of sympathy and love,
Servant of parted friends,
Consoler of the lonely,
Bond of the scattered
family, Enlarger of
the common life.

- - - - - - - - - - - - - - - -

CHARLES WILLIAM ELIOT

Inscription on former post office, now Smithsonian
National Postal Museum, Washington, D.C.

There are **HUNDREDS** *of ways to* **KNEEL AND KISS** *the* *ground.*

—

RUMI

IN TIMES OF **JOY,** ALL OF US WISHED WE POSSESSED **A TAIL WE COULD WAG.**

———

W. H. AUDEN

I stand here today, **GRATEFUL FOR** the diversity of my heritage, aware that my parents' dreams live on in my precious daughters. I stand here knowing that my story is part of the larger American story, that I owe a debt **TO ALL OF THOSE WHO CAME BEFORE ME,** and that, in no other country on earth, is my story possible.

BARACK OBAMA

YOU CAN'T APPRECIATE HOME TILL YOU'VE LEFT IT,
money till it's spent …,
nor old Glory till you see it
hanging on a broomstick on
the shanty of a consul in
a foreign town.

—

O. HENRY

A single act of kindness throws out roots in all directions, and the roots spring up and make new trees.

—

Father Frederick William Faber

A TREE IS KNOWN BY ITS FRUIT;
a man by his deeds.
A good deed is never lost;
he who sows courtesy
reaps friendship, and
HE WHO PLANTS KINDNESS
GATHERS LOVE.

—

ST. BASIL the GREAT

Parents are friends
that life gives us.

Friends are
parents the heart
chooses.

—

Comtesse Diane

A friend is a present you give to yourself.

—

ATTRIBUTED TO
Robert Louis Stevenson

DEAR MR. VON FUEHLSDORFF:

Thank you for your champagne. It arrived.

I drank it, and I was gayer.

Thanks again.

Letter from actress **MARILYN MONROE** to Volkmar von Fuehlsdorff, the German consulate general, February 17, 1962

A man must **THANK HIS DEFECTS** and stand in some **TERROR OF HIS TALENTS.**

—

RALPH WALDO EMERSON

I AM GRATEFUL

for **MY VICTORIES,**
but I am especially
grateful for
MY LOSSES,
because they only made me
WORK HARDER.

—

MUHAMMAD ALI

GRATITUDE

*is the inward feeling
of kindness received.*

THANKFULNESS

*is the natural impulse
to express that feeling.*

THANKSGIVING

*is the following of
that impulse.*

—

Henry Van Dyke

Gratitude is the
memory of the
heart.

—

Jean Baptiste Massieu

**I can never take for granted the
euphoria produced by a cup of**

COFFEE.

I'M GRATEFUL every day that it
isn't banned as a drug, that I don't
have to buy it from a pusher, that
its cost is minimal and there's no
need to increase the intake.

—

ANITA LOOS

Thank God for

TEA!

What would the world do
without tea?—how did it
exist? I AM GLAD I was
not born before tea.

Sydney Smith

GRATITUDE
is a quality similar
to **ELECTRICITY**:
it must be produced
and discharged and
used up in order
to exist at all.

—

WILLIAM FAULKNER

Feeling GRATITUDE and not expressing it is like wrapping a present and not giving it.

—

William Arthur Ward

You have good sense,
and a sweet temper, and
I am sure you have

a grateful heart,

that could never receive
kindness without
wishing to return it.
I do not know any better
qualifications for a
friend and companion.

—

Jane Austen

The glory of friendship is not the outstretched hand, not the kindly smile, nor the joy of companionship; it is the spiritual inspiration that comes to one when you discover that someone else believes in you and is willing to trust you with a friendship.

Ralph Waldo Emerson

Madam,

Learning that you have passed the eighty-fourth year of life, have given to the soldiers, some three hundred pairs of stockings, knitted by yourself, I wish to offer my thanks. Will you also convey my thanks to those young ladies who have done so much in feeding our soldiers while passing through your city?

Letter from **PRESIDENT ABRAHAM LINCOLN** to Mrs. Esther Stockton, July 8, 1864

*As we express
our gratitude, we must
never forget that*

THE HIGHEST
APPRECIATION
IS NOT TO
UTTER WORDS,
BUT TO
LIVE BY THEM.

—

JOHN F. KENNEDY

Gratitude
takes three forms:

**a feeling
in the heart,**

**an expression
in words,**

**and a giving
in return.**

—

John Wanamaker

COOKING

is a caring and
nurturing act.
It's kind of
the ultimate gift
for someone,
to cook for them.

—

Curtis Stone

DINING

with one's friends
and beloved family
is certainly one of
life's primal and
most innocent
delights, one that is
both soul-satisfying
and eternal.

—

Julia Child

Those who bring
SUNSHINE into the lives
of others cannot keep it
from themselves.

—

J. M. BARRIE

Kindness is like **SNOW.**
It beautifies everything
it covers.

—

Kahlil Gibran

IN REAL FRIENDSHIP
*the judgment,
the genius,
the prudence
of each party*
**BECOME THE
COMMON PROPERTY
OF BOTH.**

—

Maria Edgeworth

The
CONNECTIONS
we make in the
course of a life—
maybe that's what
HEAVEN is.

—

FRED ROGERS

—

One can
pay back the
loan of gold, but
**ONE DIES
FOREVER
IN DEBT**
to those who
are kind.

—

MALAYAN PROVERB

What we have done for ourselves alone, dies with us; what we have done for others and the world, **REMAINS AND IS IMMORTAL.**

—

ALBERT PIKE

Beware

of writing to me.
I always answer.
My father spent
the last 20 years
of his life
writing letters.
If someone

thanked him for a present, he thanked them for thanking him and there was no end to the exchange but death.

Letter from writer **EVELYN WAUGH** to Lady Mosley (formerly Diana Mitford), March 30, 1966

GRATITUDE is not only
THE GREATEST
OF VIRTUES,
but the parent of all others.

—

CICERO

For all that has been,

THANK YOU.

For all that is to come,

"YES!"

—

Dag Hammarskjöld

UNION SQUARE & CO. and the distinctive
Union Square & Co. logo are trademarks of
Sterling Publishing Co., Inc.

**UNION
SQUARE
& CO.**

NEW YORK

Union Square & Co., LLC, is a subsidiary of
Sterling Publishing Co., Inc.

Text compilation © 2023 ROBIE LLC

Illustrations © 2023 Union Square & Co., LLC

ISBN 978-1-4549-4852-0

For information about custom editions, special sales,
and premium purchases, please contact specialsales@
unionsquareandco.com.

Printed in China

2 4 6 8 10 9 7 5 3 1

unionsquareandco.com

Cover and Interior Design by Joe Newton & Maria Clavijo

Thanks is given to the Zora Neale Hurston Trust and
Victoria Sanders & Associates for permission to quote
from Zora Neale Hurston's letter to Cornelia Chapin,
February 29, 1932.

Thanks is also given to Kim Holden for permission to
include her quote.